Kids Can Draw

ANIMAL FUN

ISBN-13: 978-0-7607-7406-9
ISBN-10: 0-7607-7406-4

Printed and bound in China

07 08 09 10 MCH 10 9 8 7 6 5 4 3

Walter Foster is a registered trademark.

Original titles *J'apprends à dessiner les animaux de la forêt* and
J'apprends à dessiner les animaux de la maison,
© 1992 Editions Fleurus, Paris

Kids Can Draw
ANIMAL FUN

by Philippe Legendre

BACKPACKBOOKS

NEW YORK

CONTENTS

Attention Parents and Teachers

All children can draw a circle, a square, or a triangle . . . which means that they can also learn to draw a bear, a squirrel, a fish, or a parakeet! The KIDS CAN DRAW learning method is easy and fun. Children will learn a technique and a vocabulary of shapes that will form the basis for all kinds of drawing.

Pictures are created by combining geometric shapes to form a mass of volumes and surfaces. From this stage, children can give character to their sketches with straight, curved, or broken lines.

With just a few strokes of the pencil, a favorite animal will appear—and with the addition of color, the picture will be a real work of art!

The KIDS CAN DRAW method offers a real apprenticeship in technique and a first look at composition, proportion, shapes, and lines. The simplicity of this method ensures that the pleasure of drawing is always the most important factor.

About Philippe Legendre

French painter, engraver, and illustrator, Philippe Legendre also runs a school of art for children aged 6–14 years. Legendre frequently spends time in schools and has developed this method of learning so that all children can discover the artist within themselves.

Helpful Tips

1. Each picture is made up of simple geometric shapes, which are illustrated at the top of the left-hand page. This is called the **Vocabulary of Shapes.** Encourage children to practice drawing each shape before starting their pictures.

2. Suggest children use a pencil to do their sketches. This way, if they don't like a particular shape, they can just erase it and try again.

3. A dotted line indicates that the line should be erased. Have children draw the whole shape and then erase the dotted part of the line.

4. Once children finish their drawings, they can color them with crayons, colored pencils, or felt-tip markers. They may want to go over the lines with a black pencil or pen.

Now let's get started!

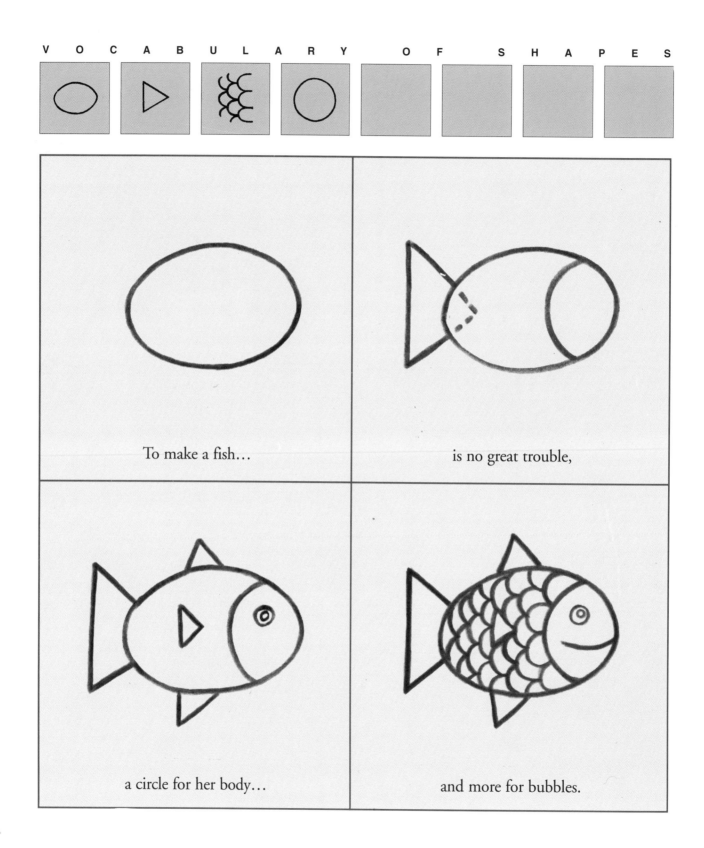

To make a fish…

is no great trouble,

a circle for her body…

and more for bubbles.

Fish

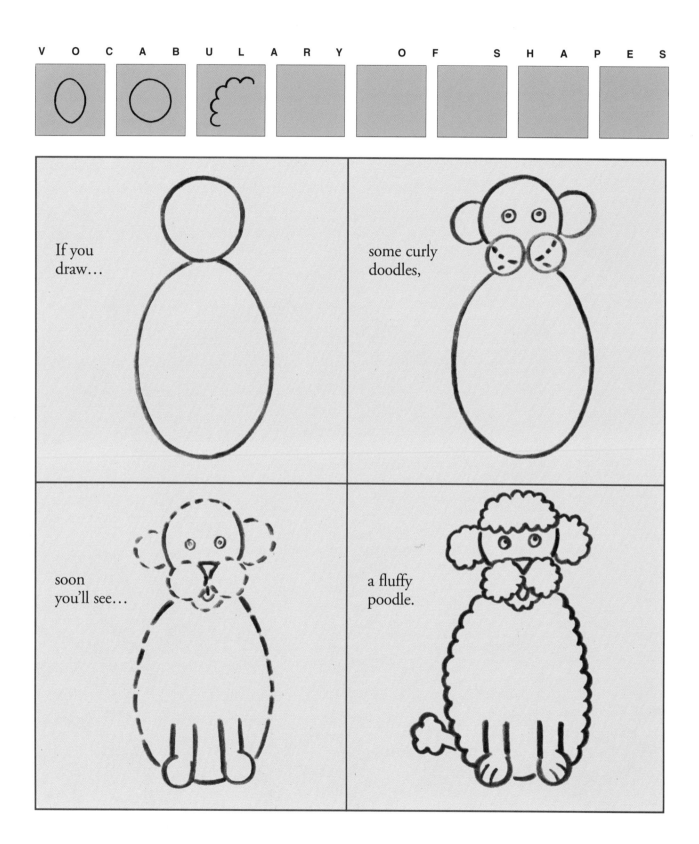

If you draw…

some curly doodles,

soon you'll see…

a fluffy poodle.

Poodle

A circle makes…

the head atop…

a bunny that…

goes hippity-hop.

Bunny

You can almost hear the cat purr,

when you draw stripes…

on her fur.

Cat

His bumpy shell…

with squares is packed.

He carries his home…

upon his back.

Turtle

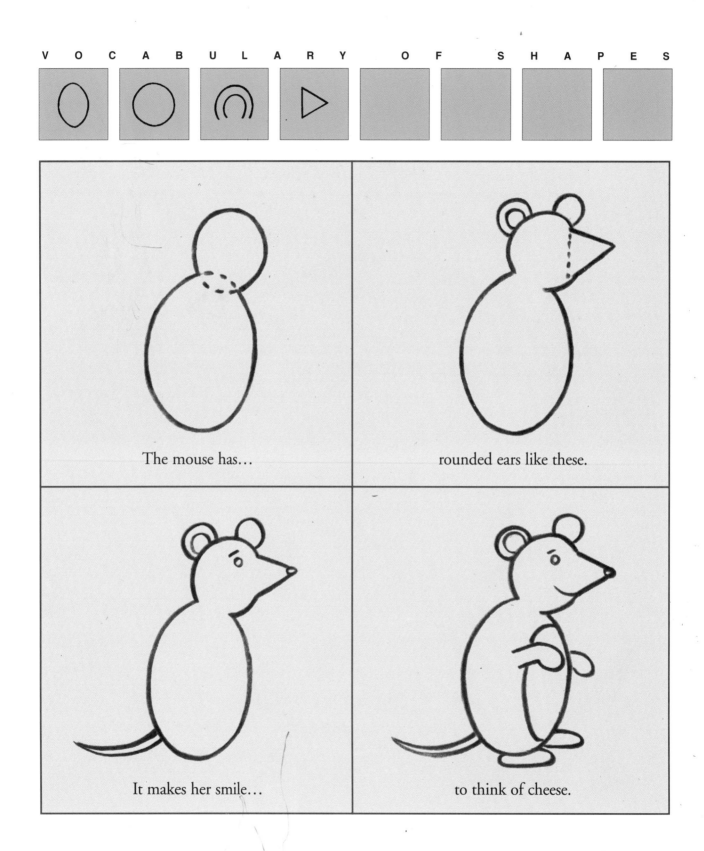

The mouse has...

rounded ears like these.

It makes her smile...

to think of cheese.

Mouse

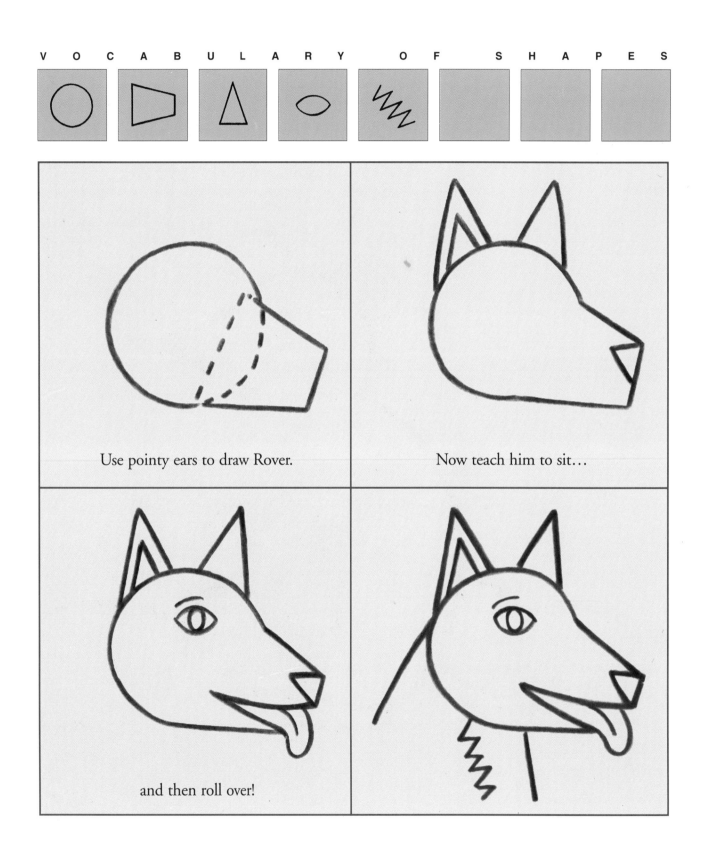

Use pointy ears to draw Rover.

Now teach him to sit…

and then roll over!

Dog

To draw this furry fellow,

make a half-circle big.

But don't draw a curly tail—

he's not a real pig!

Guinea Pig

This brightly colored bird…

has triangles for feet.

"Polly wants a cracker,"

says the parakeet.

Parakeet

At last, you can draw your favorite pets—from a trusty dog to a little mouse.

Now make a pretty picture of them living in your house.

The round bear hunts for honey…

in hives up in the trees.

With his thick and shaggy coat,

he doesn't mind the bees.

Bear

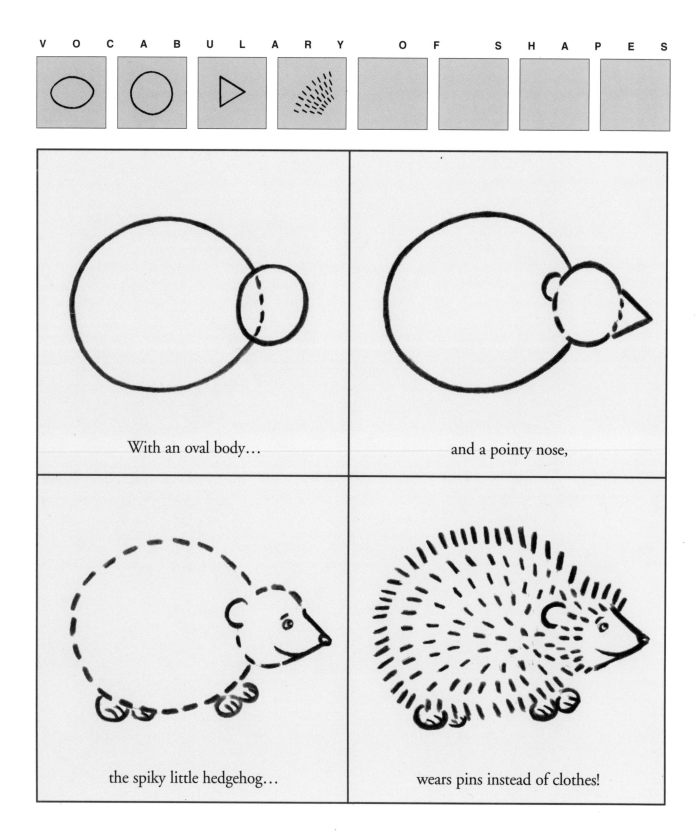

With an oval body…

and a pointy nose,

the spiky little hedgehog…

wears pins instead of clothes!

Hedgehog

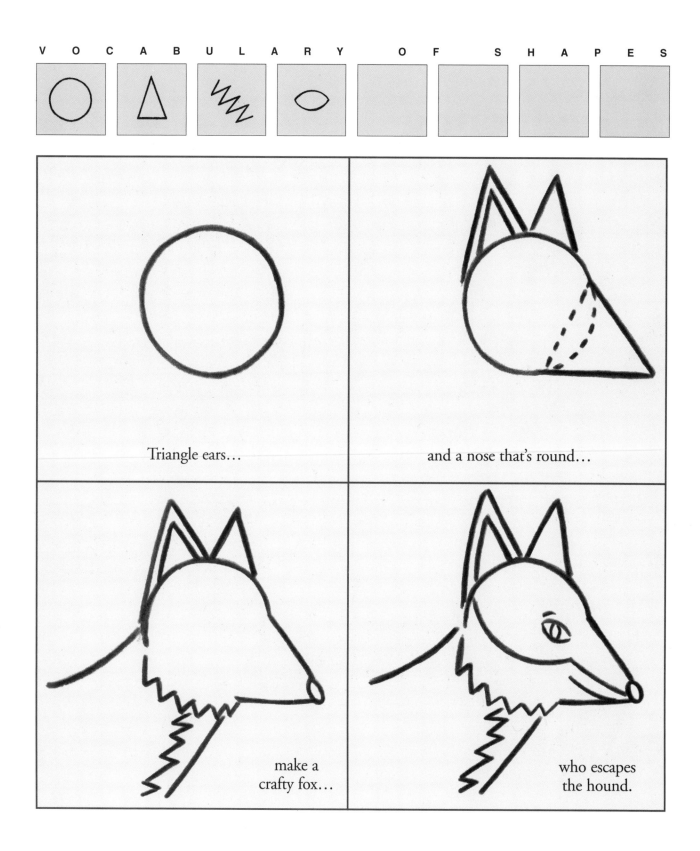

Triangle ears...

and a nose that's round...

make a
crafty fox...

who escapes
the hound.

Fox

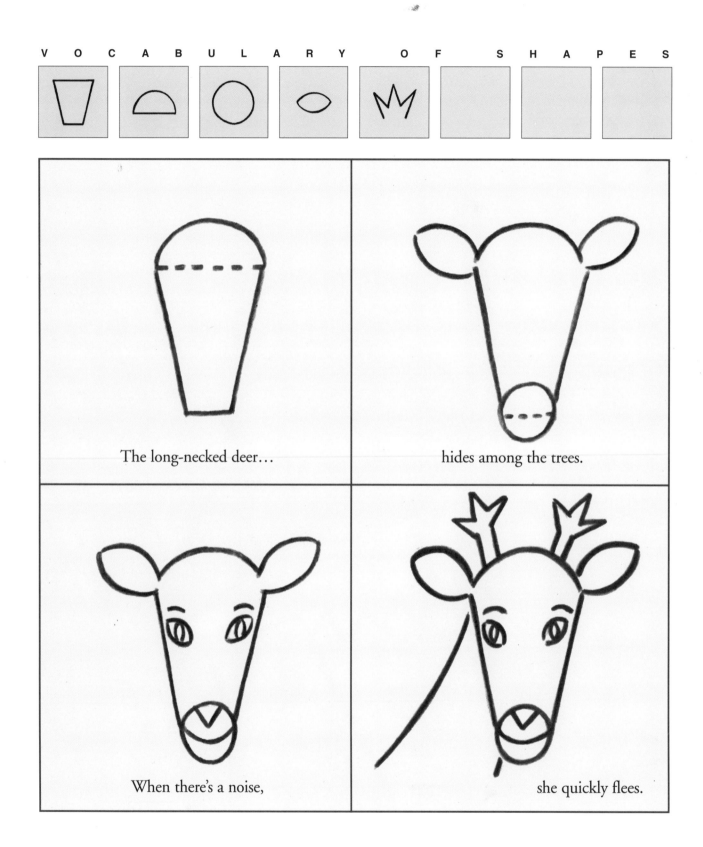

The long-necked deer…

hides among the trees.

When there's a noise,

she quickly flees.

Deer

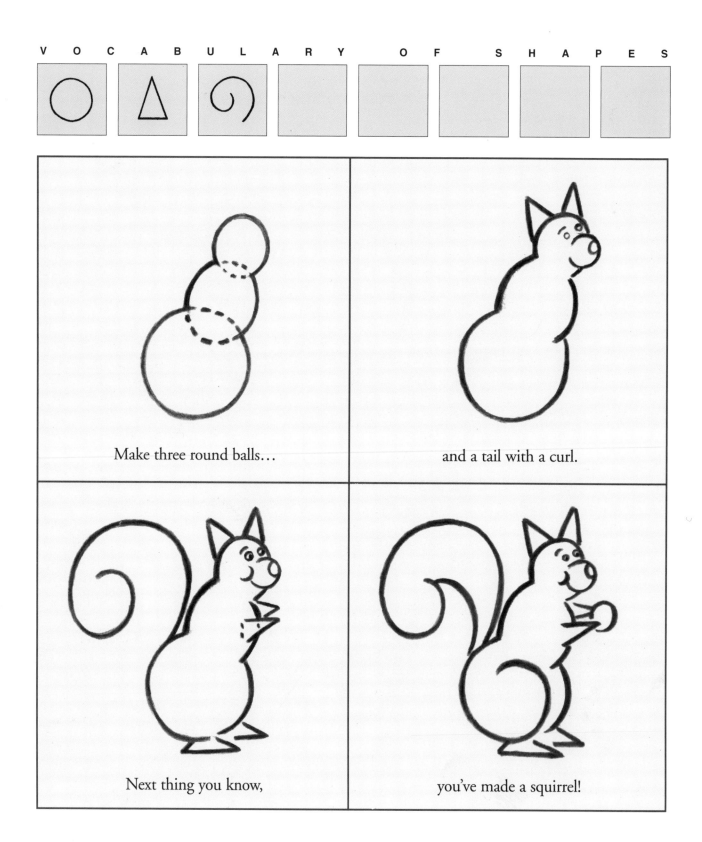

Make three round balls…

and a tail with a curl.

Next thing you know,

you've made a squirrel!

Squirrel

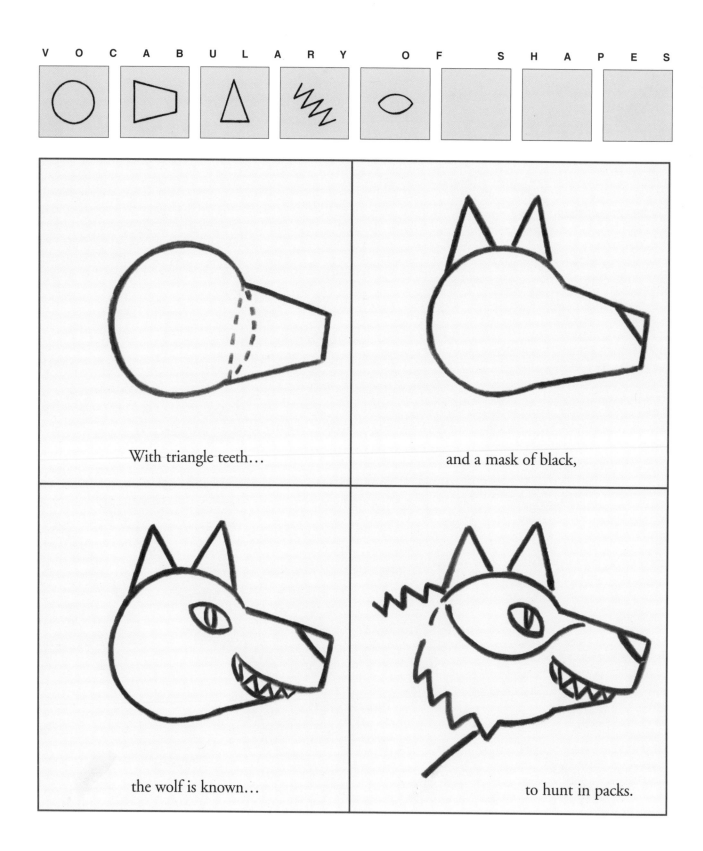

With triangle teeth…

and a mask of black,

the wolf is known…

to hunt in packs.

Wolf

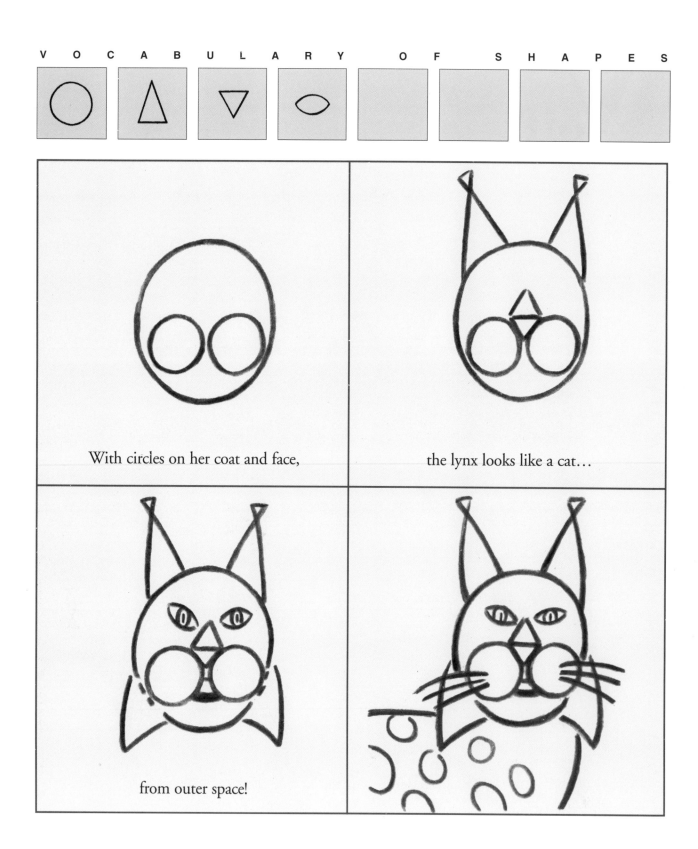

With circles on her coat and face,

the lynx looks like a cat…

from outer space!

40

Lynx

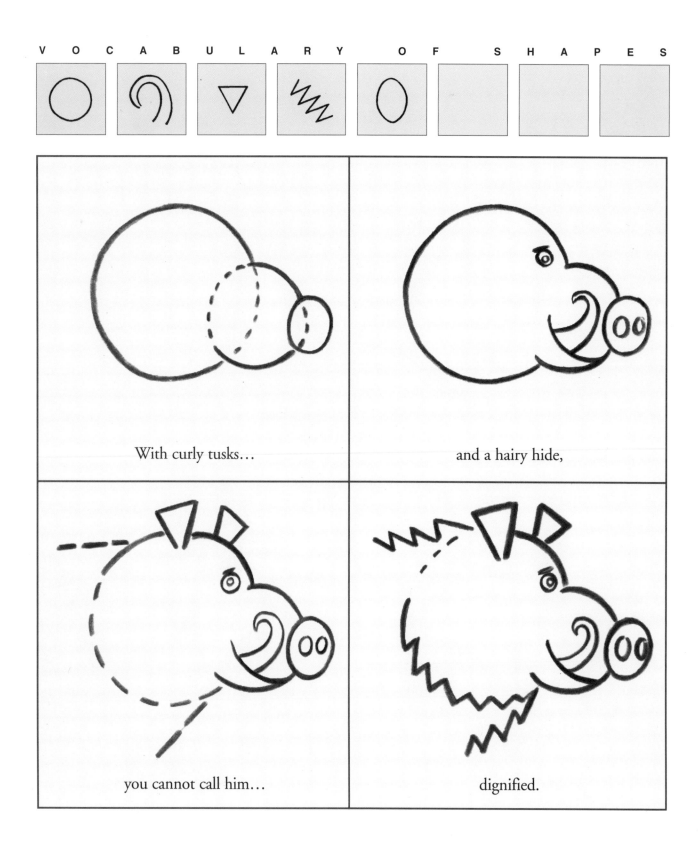

With curly tusks…

and a hairy hide,

you cannot call him…

dignified.

Wild **B**oar

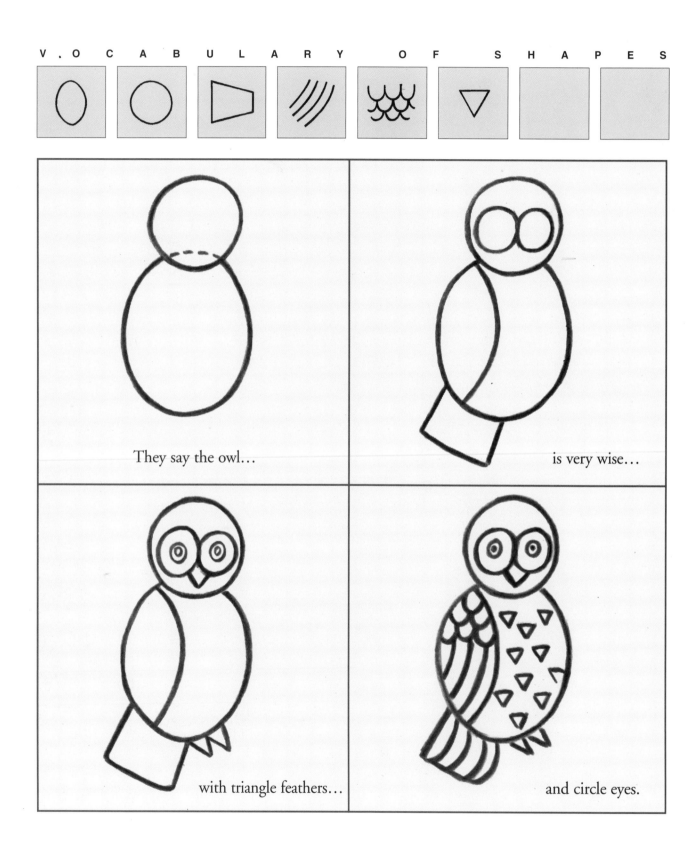

They say the owl…

is very wise…

with triangle feathers…

and circle eyes.

Owl

In the forest you have drawn, the animals are on the prowl.

You can make the wise owl hoot and the fierce wolf growl.